A Lifetime
of
Limericks

By Clive Ottley

Images under licence from Shutterstock.
Text copyright 2024 Clive Ottley.
Edited and designed by Carol Mitchell for CaribbeanReads.
ISBN: 978-1-953747-29-7

This book is dedicated to my entire immediate family.

To my dear wife, Carmen, for listening to and commenting on my work; to our daughter Carol and her husband Wayne, for believing I could do this, and for making it happen; and to our grandchildren, Andrew and Lex, who challenged me to send them a new limerick every week. I did not always keep up, but some of these verses are the result of that challenge.

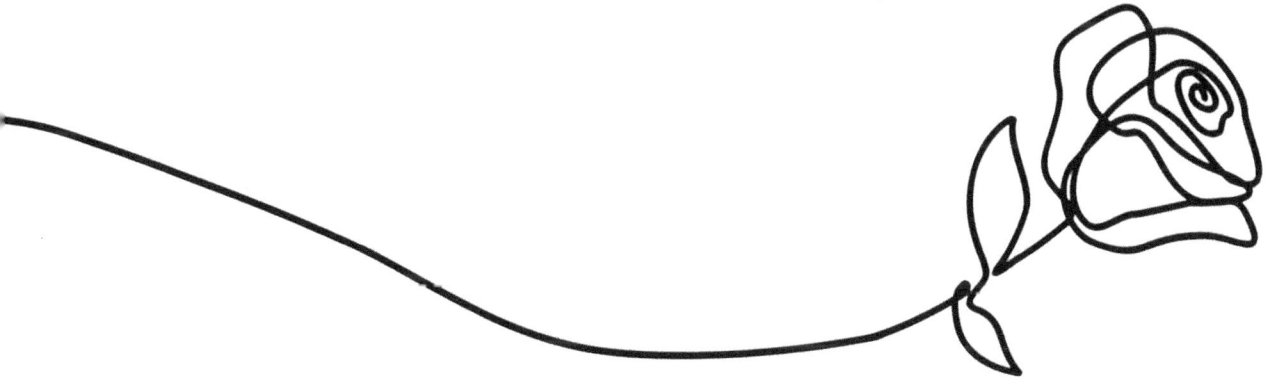

Table of Contents

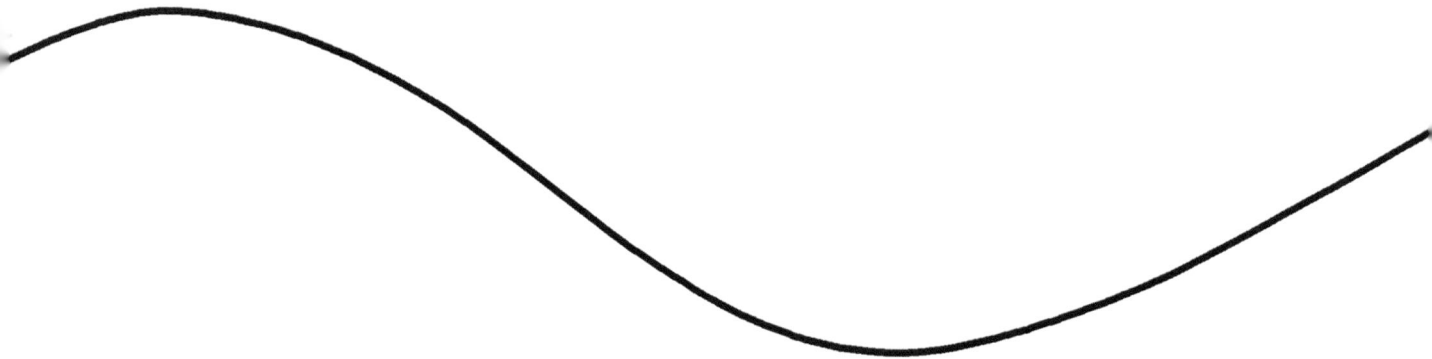

Animals

If while you are sauntering by,

Bird poop falls on you from the sky.

Don't ask why it fell on you

Or if it will smell on you.

Just be thankful that dogs cannot fly.

The majestic elephant shows

No finesse, no deftness, no pose.

But the lowly opposum

Can pick up a blossom

'Cause it has opposable toes.

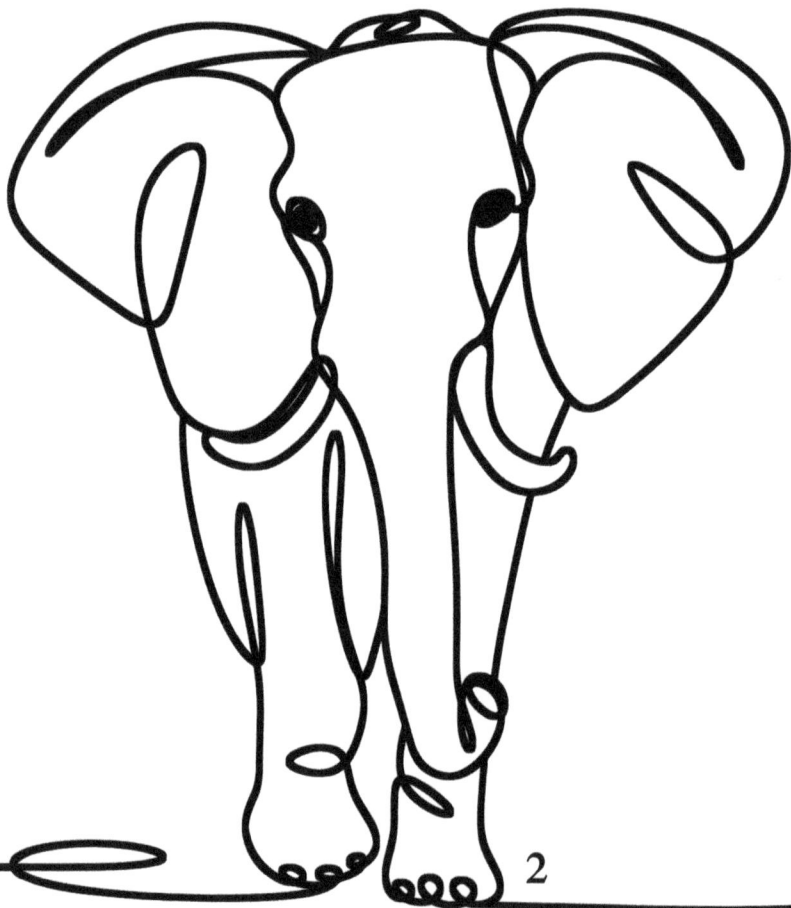

2

The monkey, both female and male,

When eating fresh fruit (never stale),

Can put bits in his jaws

Without using his paws

'Cause he has a prehensile tail.

On getting the worm

The early bird has much appeal.

Folks cite its industry with zeal.

But don't become surly

The worm too was early,

And he ended up as a meal.

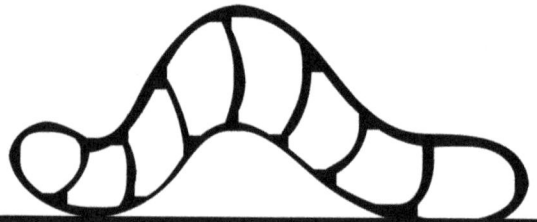

The early bird, many folks state

Is a creature we should emulate.

But 'tis my belief,

Worms won't come to grief

If they stayed in 'til well after eight.

The early bird, many folks state

Is a creature we should emulate.

But sloth has its charm.

Worms would suffer no harm

If they lingered in bed until eight.

The early bird down from the trees

Devoured the slow worm with ease.

But, the first mouse took the rap

He was caught in the trap

And the second mouse he got the cheese.

Life

I said to my teen-age son Matthew

"Don't fret at the things life throws at you.

What e'er your religion

You'll oft be the pigeon

And other times you'll be the statue."

There was a young lady named Jade

Of life's problems she was not afraid.

When life served her roses

She struck happy poses.

When lemons she made lemonade.

Just for Fun

If ever your pinky gets cut

Don't suck on it. Keep your mouth shut.

For microbes may linger

 On thumb or on finger

If you have been scratching your butt.

At the annual insomnia convention

I asked the Grand Master John Pencheon:

"Do you ever sleep well?"

He said "That I can't tell.

When I do sleep I don't pay attention."

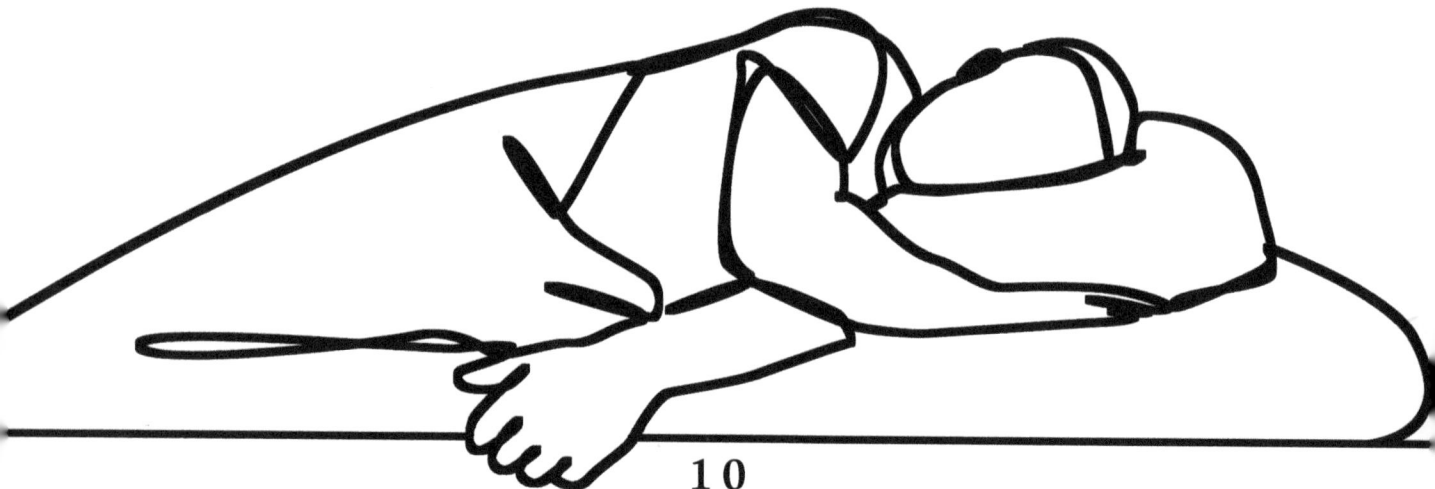

In the halls where old documents lay,

It's recorded that Confucius say:

"Man who have running nose

And who have smelling toes,

He live upside down every day."

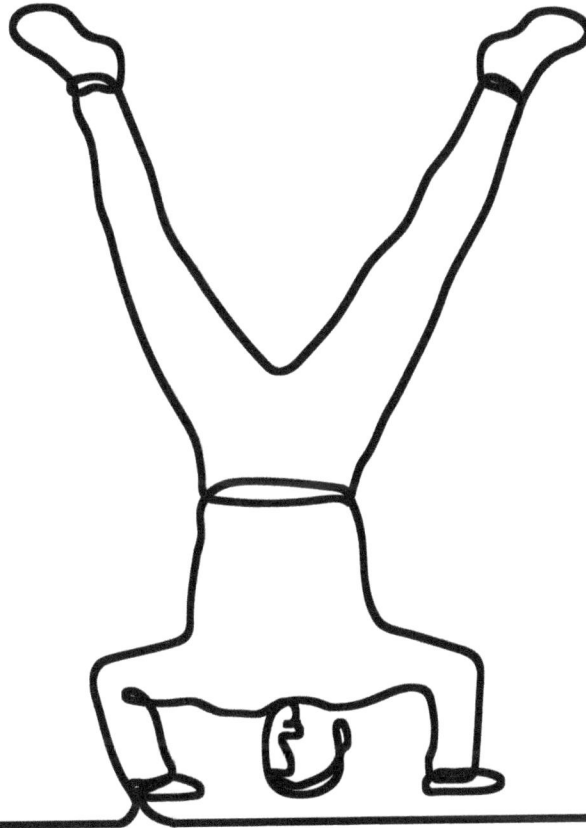

"My only child couldn't stand children.

I begged, but he firmly banned children.

To get joy in my life,

I wed a young wife,

And am making my own grandchildren.

He bought clothing, an iPhone, some wine,

And finished his shopping by nine.

"Dear, where is the car."

She said "This is bizarre.

There's no car.

    You are shopping online."

There are no bright rays on the dome,

No glittering light on the foam.

The sky is all grey.

It seems that today,

The sun will be working from home.

When this miser, a rich man's rich daughter,

Was finally convinced that she oughta

Donate to the pool

At the neighborhood school,

She gave them a large glass of water.

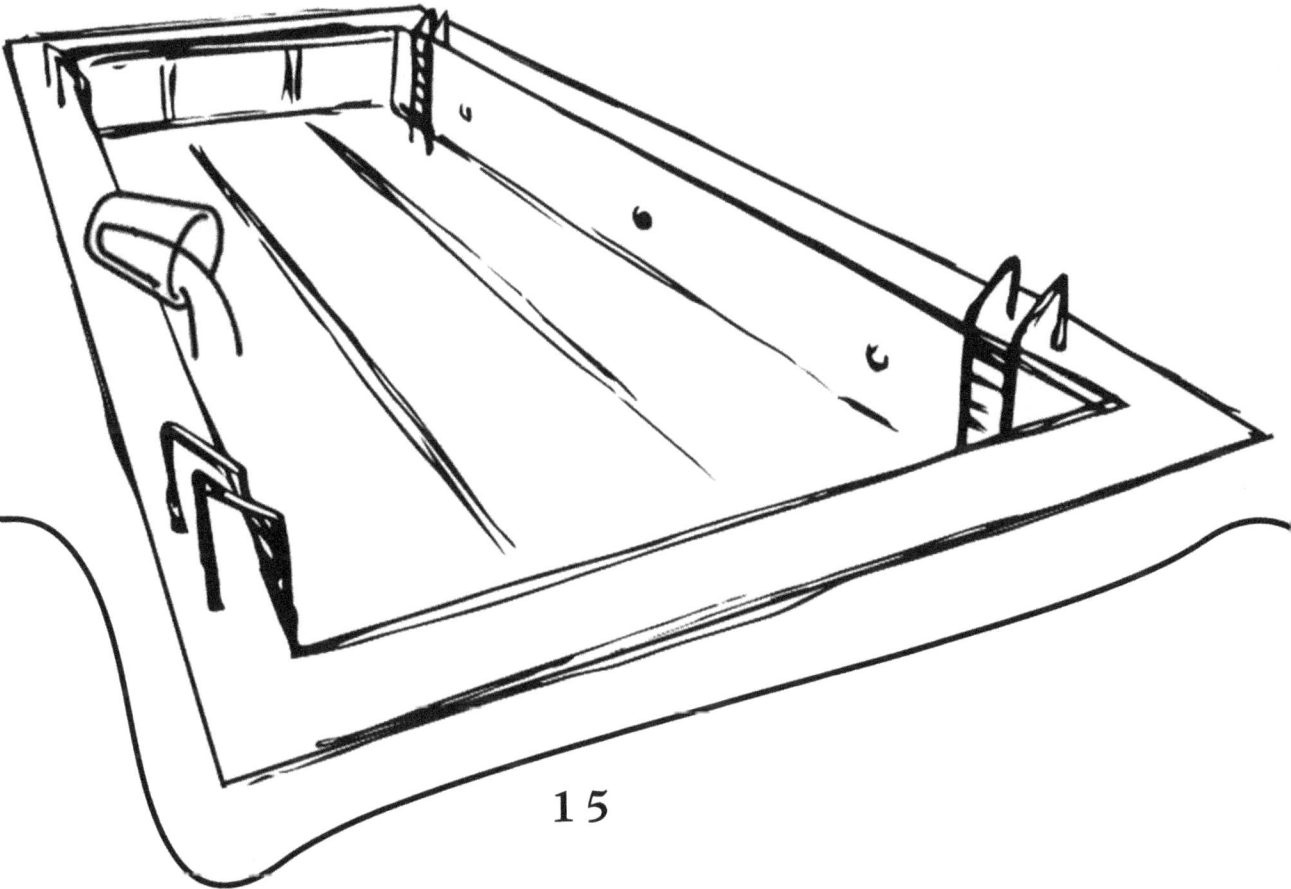

The new jigsaw puzzle stumped Mabel.

She called me to check the box label.

What I saw made me tremble.

She was trying to assemble

Some corn flakes spread out on the table.

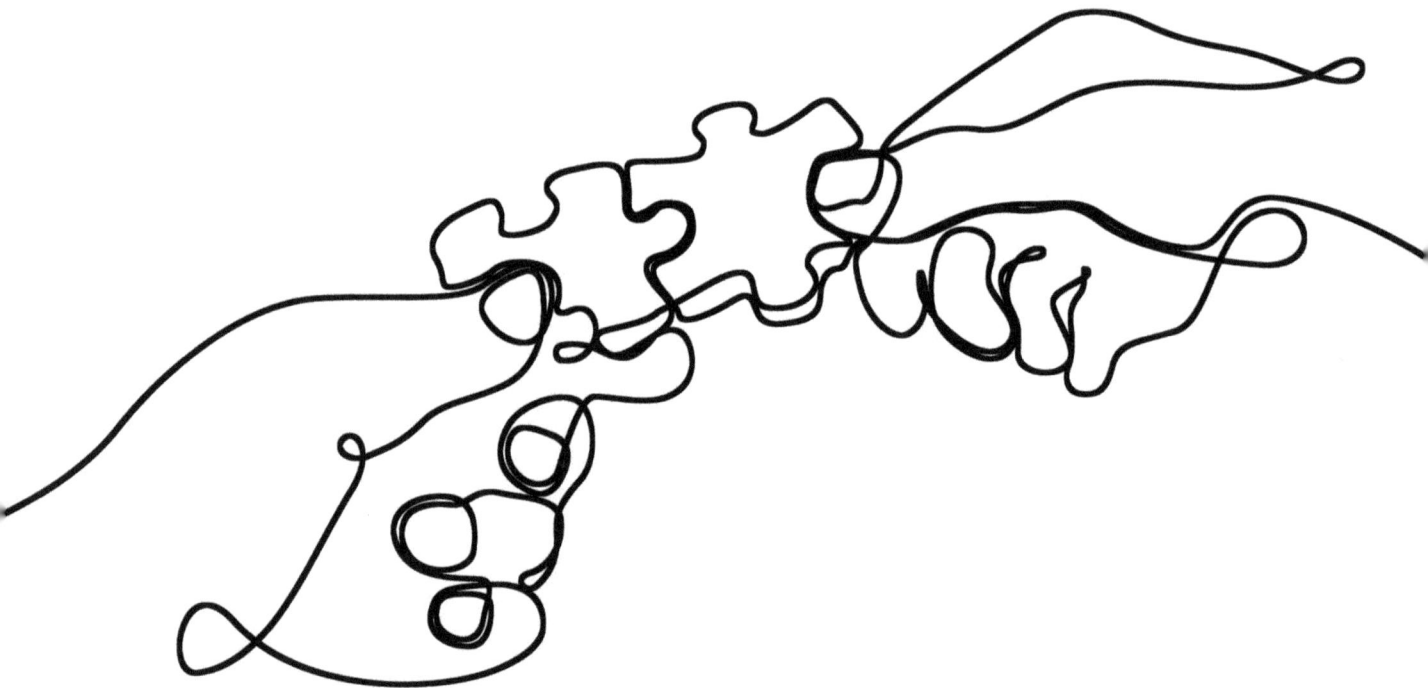

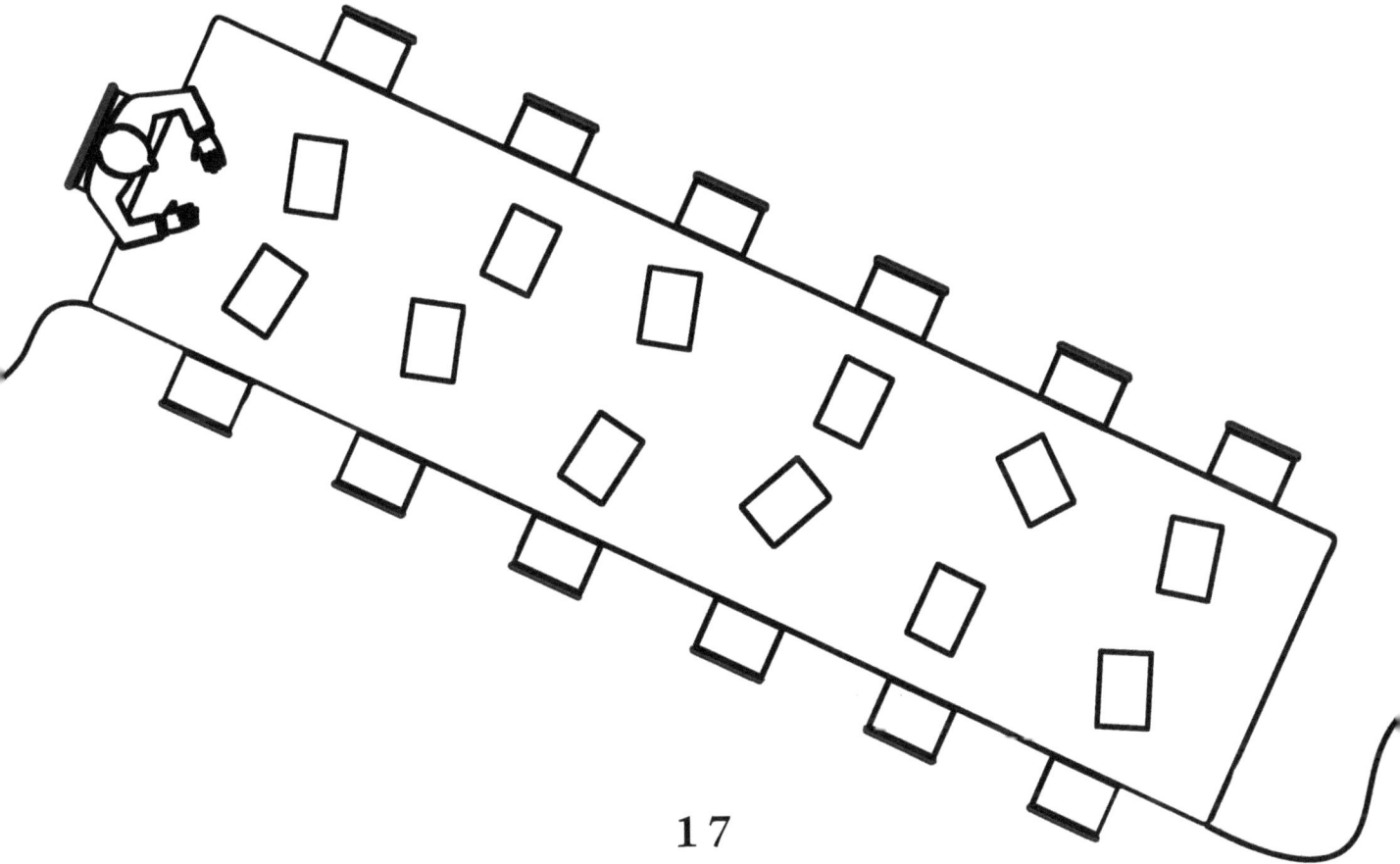

I'm a self-employed man, so no cheating.

No wrangling, no jostling for seating.

You may think I'm a nut

Talking to myself, but

I am having an urgent staff meeting.

Spinster Maud, seeing John as he eyed

Her pink undies hung out to be dried

Said "Perhaps there's no harm meant,

But if you touch one garment,

You'll have to take me as your bride."

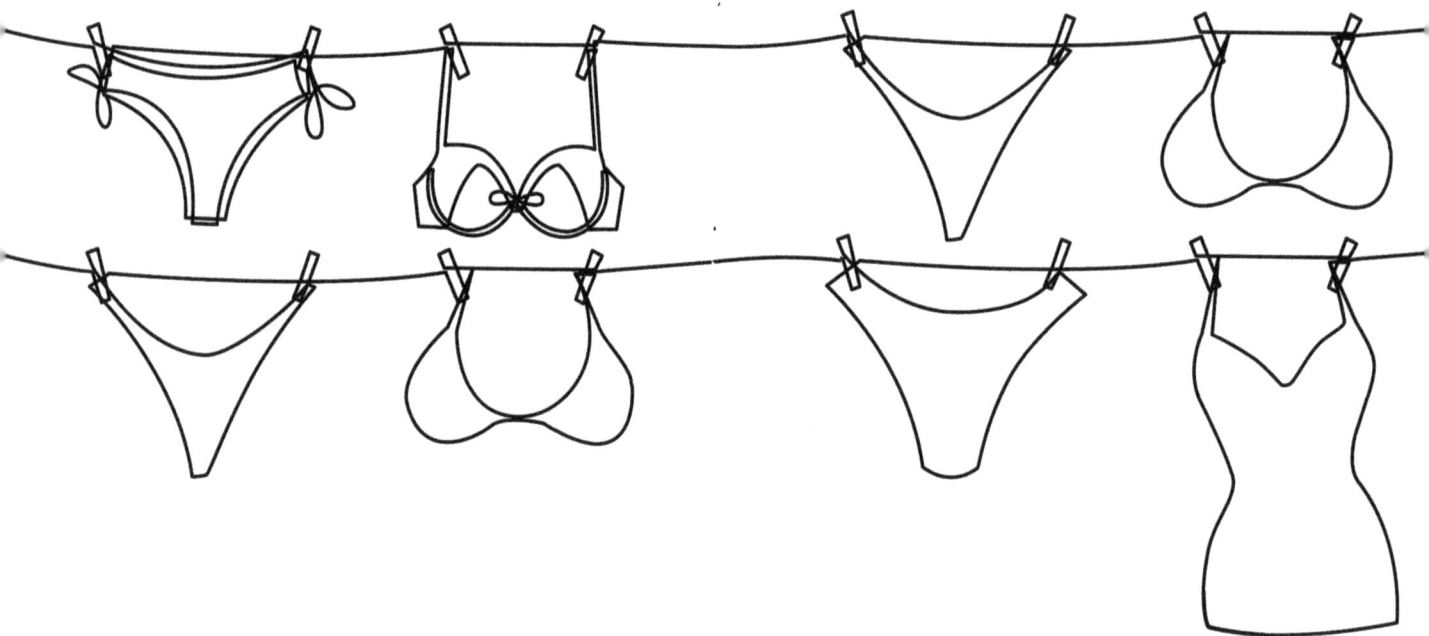

Jonathan, when away from his duties,

Spends his time with twelve dazzling beauties.

He claims each of the dozen

Is really his cousin,

But everyone knows what the truth is.

A new pugilist, Tiger Teal

Lost his carefully-staged crowd appeal.

Bulging pecs and firm abs

Scoffed at punches and jabs

But his head was his Achilles heel.

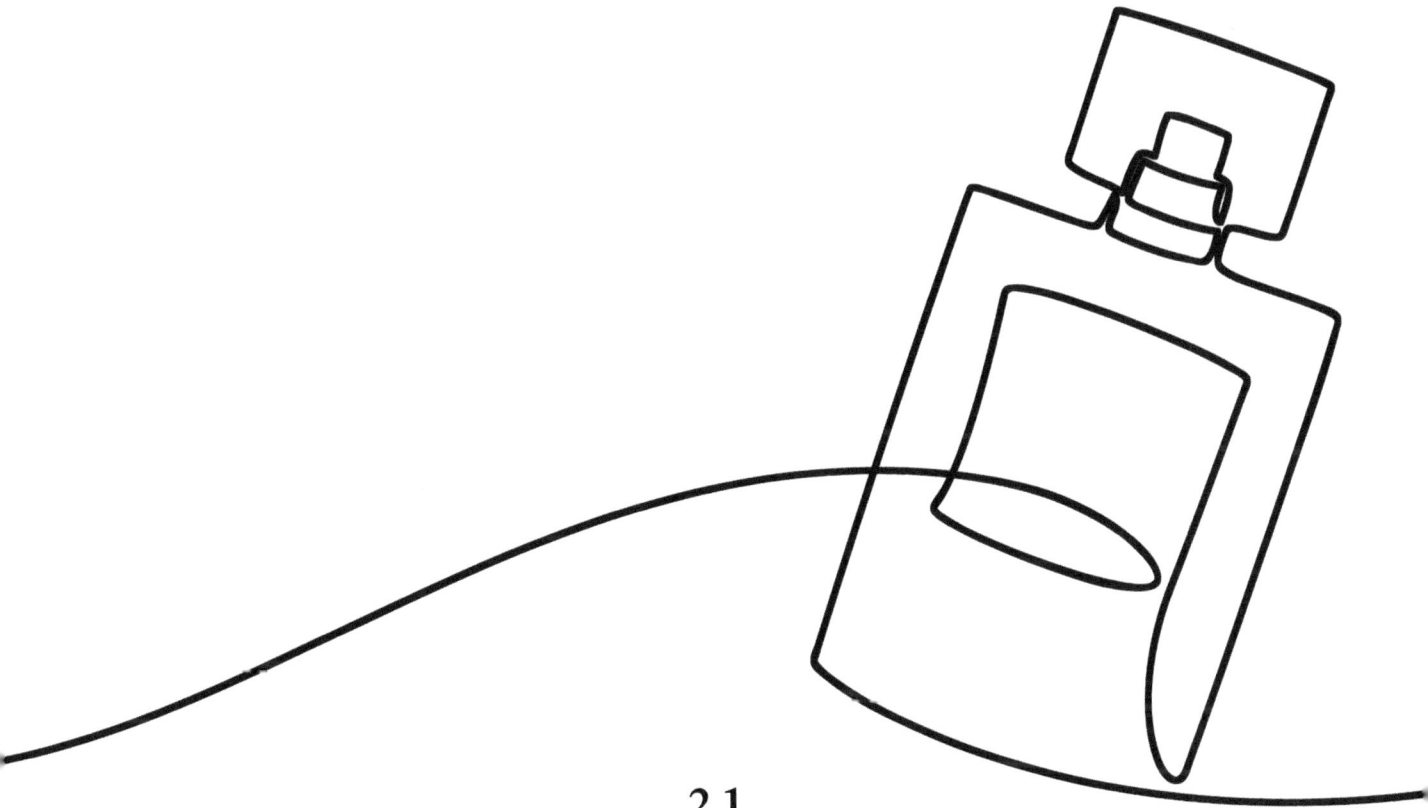

An eccentric professor from Rhone,

Rarely bathed; a fact largely unknown.

For he always dressed well,

And he disguised the smell

By strategic use of cologne.

A law abiding fellow named John

Observed the road rules; every one.

If he sat in his van

To retrieve his wife's fan,

He would first put his seat belt on.

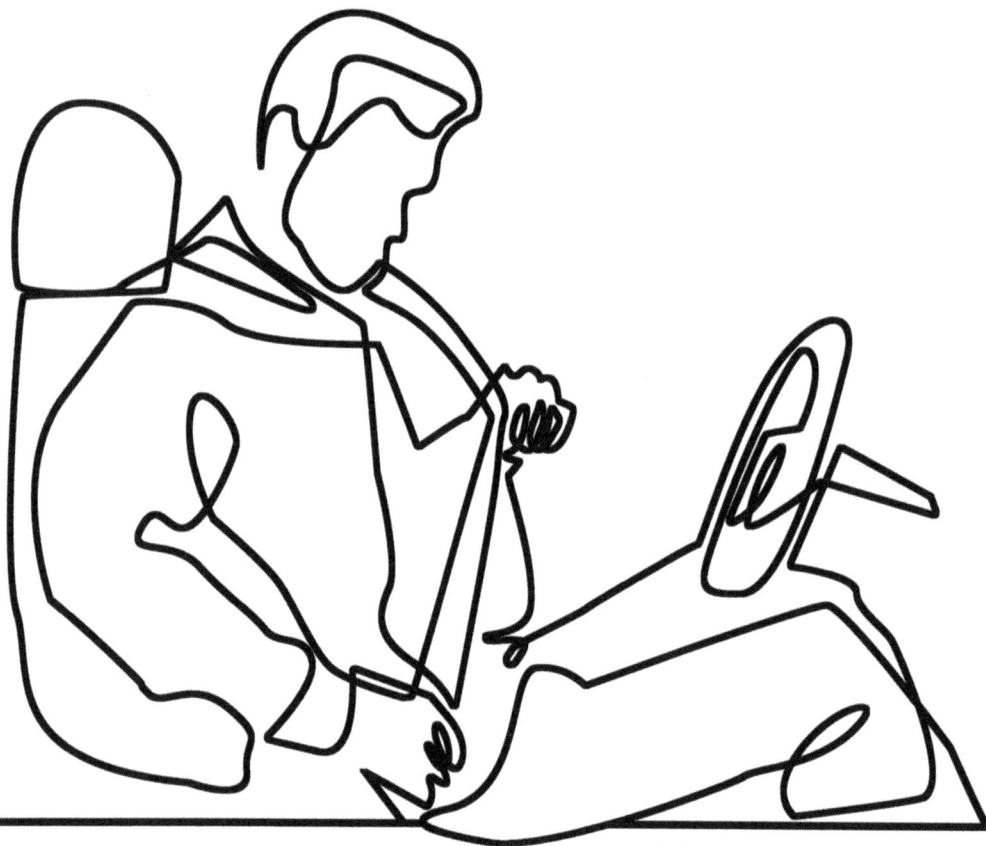

A science Professor named Wayne,

As he rushed to the bathroom in pain,

Knew that reaching his goal

Hinged on bowel control

And not on his highly-trained brain.

Matchmaker, Matchmaker, Make Me a Match

Said matchmaker to spinster: "My dear,

You'll have three new proposals this year."

"Just one. I won't wait.

For the next promised date.

I'll say 'Yes' to the first that I hear."

Said matchmaker to spinster: "My dear,

You'll have three new proposals this year."

"One only," she said,

"The first I will wed

The second I'll keep as a spare."

Said matchmaker to spinster: "My dear,

You'll have three new proposals this year."

"I'll take the first one.

He may be the worst one

But I've waited so long I don't care."

Said matchmaker to spinster: "My dear,

You'll have three new proposals this year."

"Just one" her reply.

"The first one to come by

I'll marry him right then and there.""

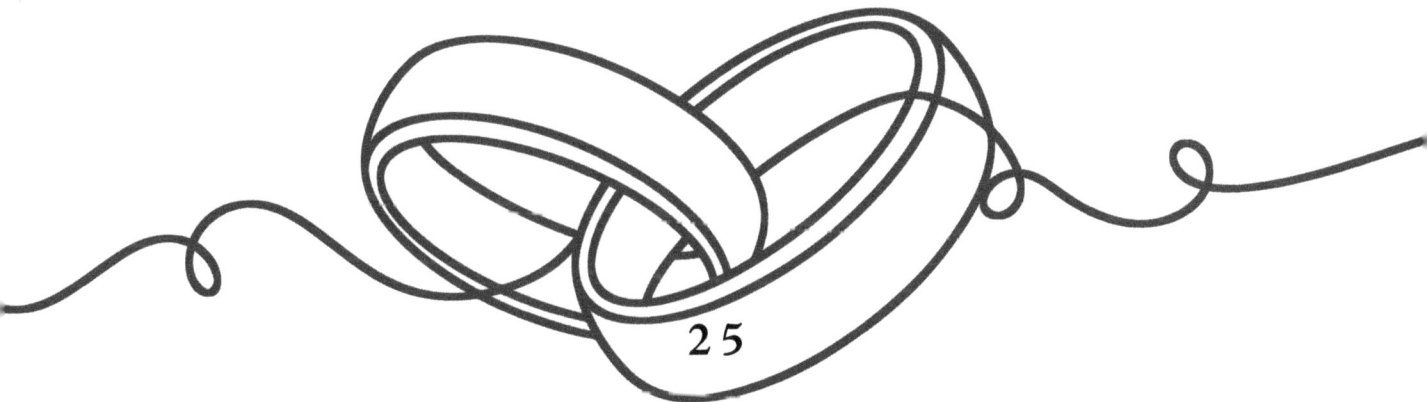

Irresistible Rhymes

Jeff Bezos the leader of Amazon

Can't sleep till he puts his pyjamas on.

It was well past ten-thirty,

His P-Js were dirty,

So he went to bed with his Mama's on.

Marge does not know what she wants in a man.

She is fine with a fat guy or thinner man

She'll take one who is penniless

She won't love him any less

A loser she'll take or a winner man

A famous King's Counsel named Gilkin,

Took the wrong bag to carry his silk in.

Judge said "Odour in court?"

So he had to report

He was using the bag he kept milk in.

Note: in the British system a successful lawyer may be made a King's or Queen's Counsel, depending on the reigning British monarch of the day. They are then entitled to wear a silk gown, often referred to simply as "silk".

There was a young father from Trinidad

Just 4 feet in height, a real mini dad

He ate tainted curry

Had intestinal hurry,

And lost so much weight he's a skinny dad.

The professor of law was distraught

Upon hearing her students were caught

By surprise when they saw

That she taught contract law.

For everyone thought she taught tort.

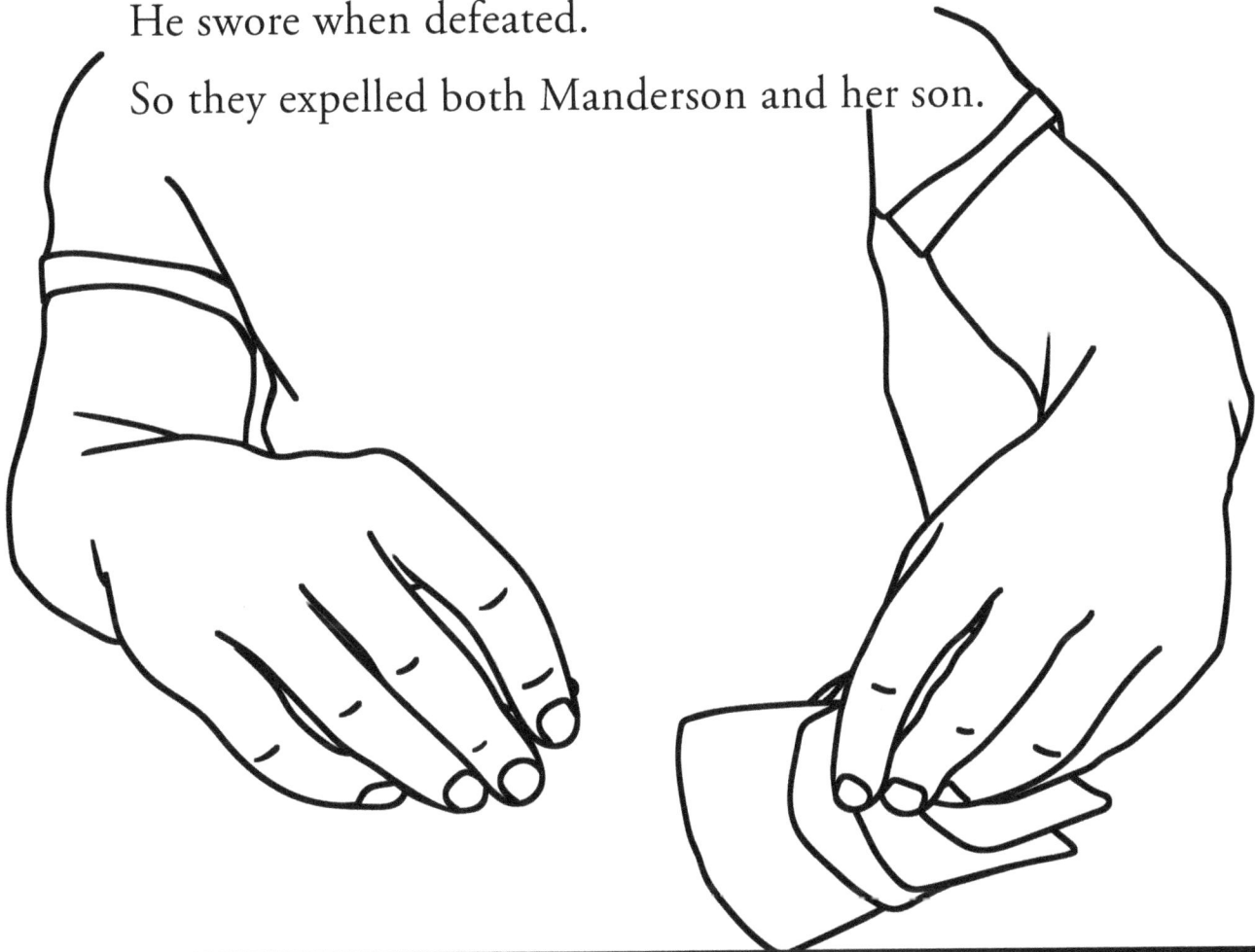

There was a bridge player named Manderson

Whose fellow club members couldn't stand her son.

He complained and he cheated,

He swore when defeated.

So they expelled both Manderson and her son.

The gluttonous Juliette Hall

Was challenged to eat at the mall:

Two burgers, three pies,

Four chicken legs with fries.

And Juliet cooly ate all.

There was a young Roman named Durius

Always in the know; always curious.

If he heard gossip late,

It was hard to placate

The furious, curious Durius.

A snooty young man named Ray Teal

Was given some fruit with his meal.

He said "Pass the knife, please.

It's not to cut cheese

The banana I'm planning to peel."

A sophomore named Seymour Fairley

Was seeing the walkway just barely.

Went back to his classes

And retrieved his glasses

And Seymour can now see more clearly.

A chronic beer bibber named Abigail
Toasted her release from the county jail.
Her friends, John and Jerry,
Each had a small sherry
But Abigail had a big ale.

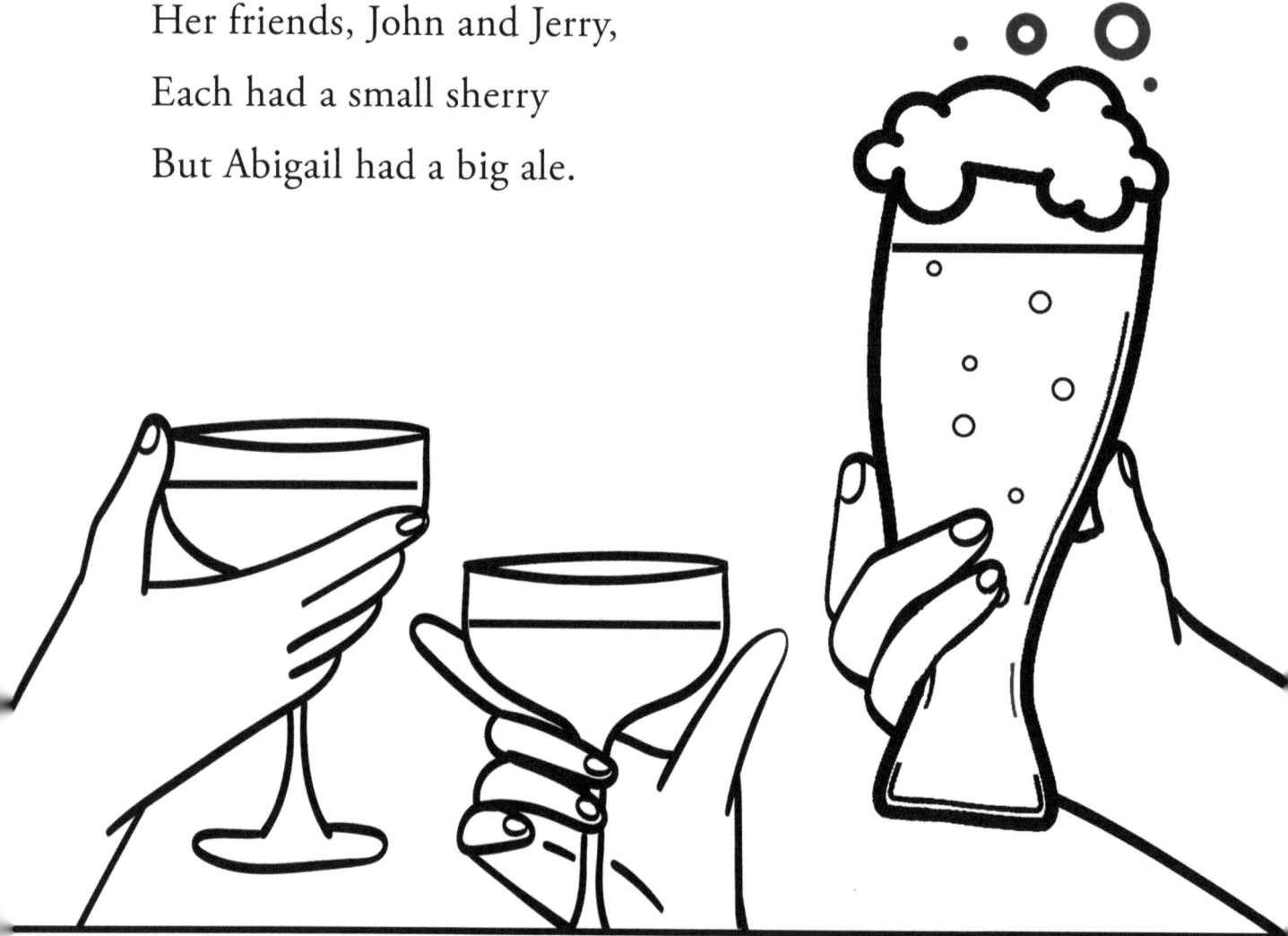

A seasoned world traveler named Everette

Ate only what folks who were clever ate.

He watched at each venue

As they queried the menu

And what they skipped Everette never ate.

A musician named Isabel Springer

Was engaged by a club as a singer.

It's become clear quite soon

That she can't turn a tune

For Isabel is a bell ringer.

A kindly landlady named Rubylette

Had one house which she wanted to be let.

Soldiers just into town

Sought a place to chow down

So they got from Rubylette a new billet.

(Note: A billet refers
to civilian premises
occupied by military
personnel.)

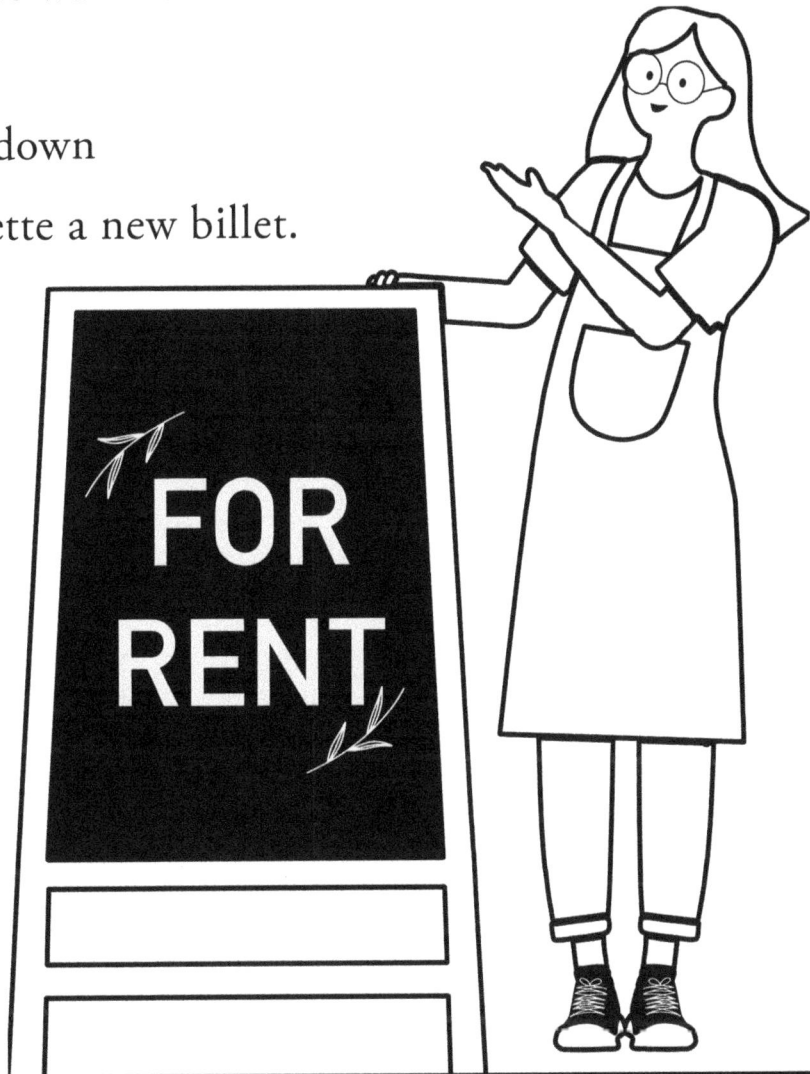

FOR RENT

A courier named Barrymore Tate

Had too much to do on his plate.

He hatched a new plan

And got his own van.

Now Barrymore can carry more freight.

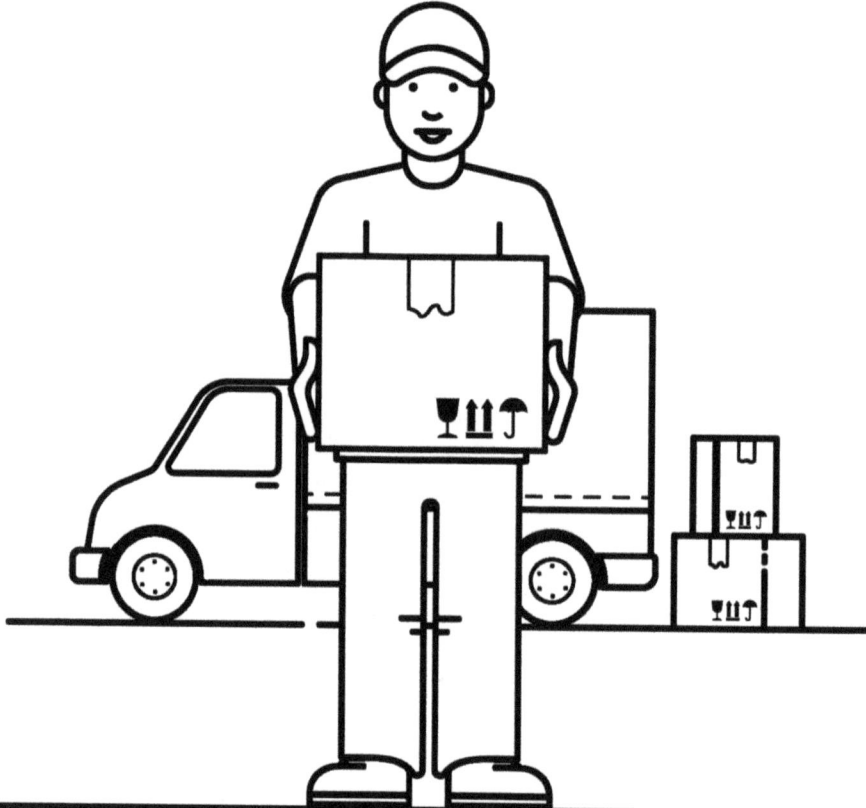

A green vervet monkey named Catherine

Awoke farmer Browne with her chattering.

His thunderous roar

As he came through the door

Sent the chattering Catherine scattering.

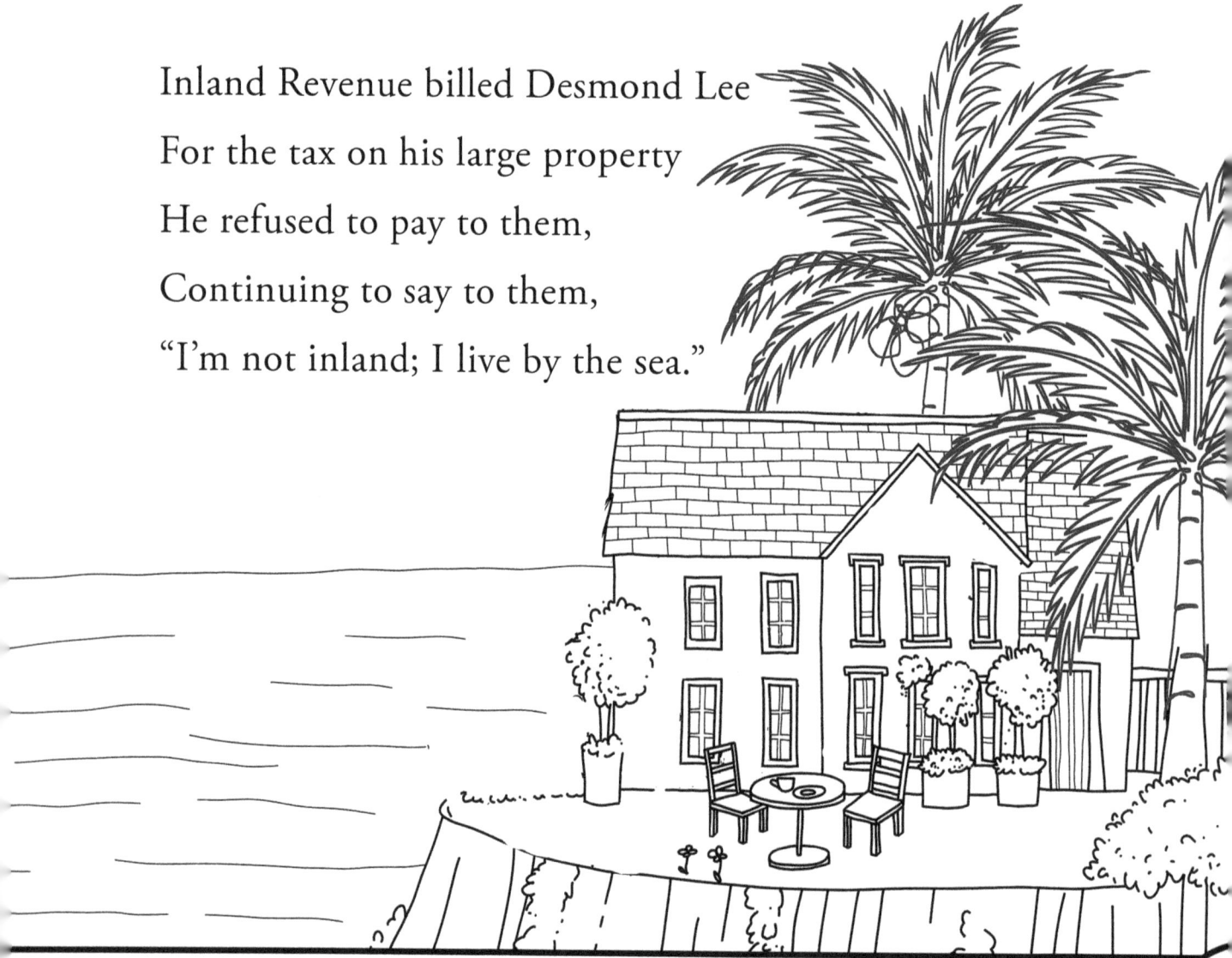

Puns

Inland Revenue billed Desmond Lee

For the tax on his large property

He refused to pay to them,

Continuing to say to them,

"I'm not inland; I live by the sea."

Jaques Costeau was filled with emotion

When he thought of the laughable notion

To pay Inland Revenue

The sum that they said was due

When he practically lived on the ocean.

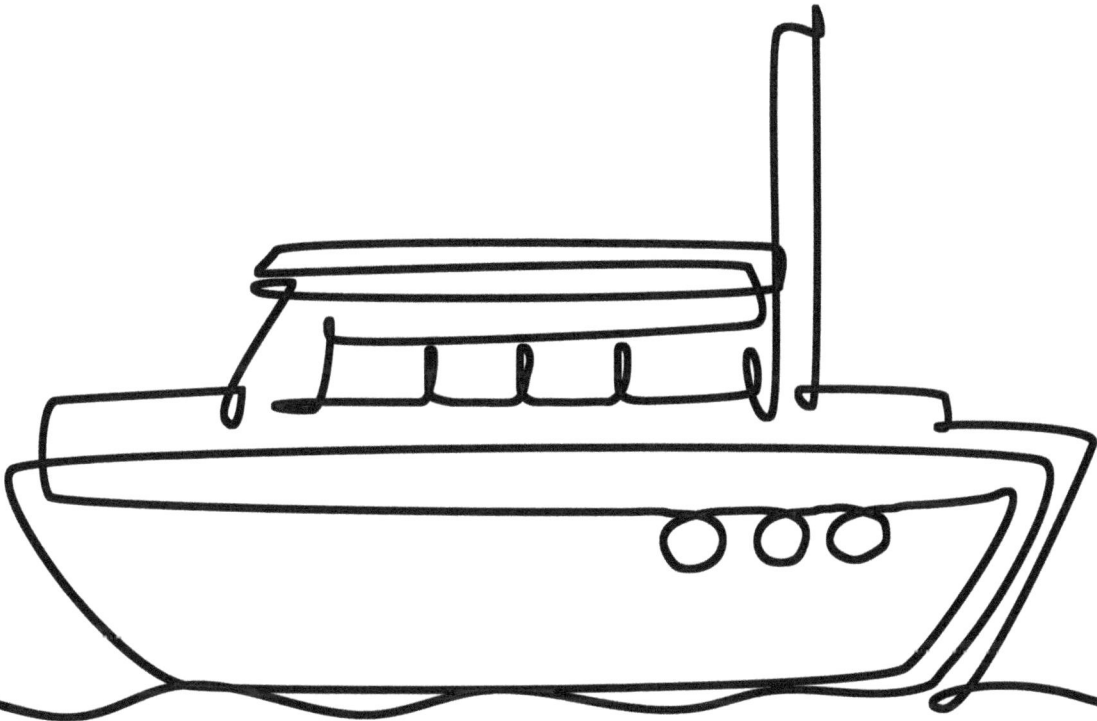

This newly wed fellow named Clyde

Set out to get lunch for his bride.

He turned back from the store

'Cause a sign on the door

Stated "No food and no drink inside."

The young mother lamented "Oh gosh,"

To her son: "Have you seen little Josh?

He's not answering to my shouts

Do you know of his whereabouts?"

"Yes mum, I put them in the wash."

A careless meat-cutter named Burke,
Who everyone knew was a jerk,
Sat, while stirring the pot,
On the slicer, and got
A little behind in his work.

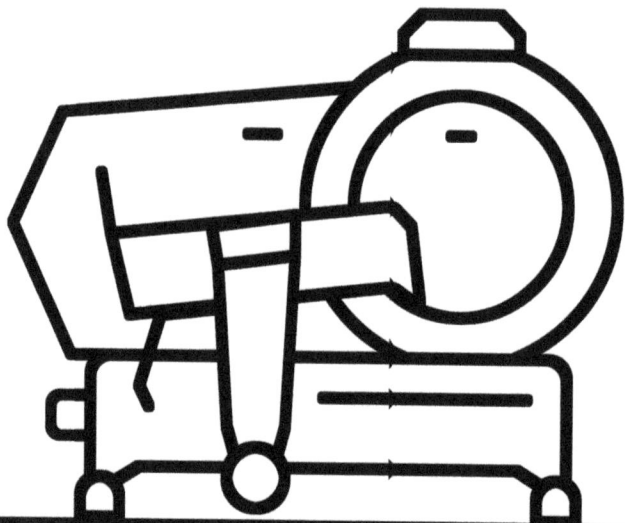

A French man named Henri LaVage

Found dead bat-ter-ies in his garage.

Stacked them up on the floor,

Hung a sign on his door.

"Please take one. They are all free of charge."

The priest saw three visitors slip

Into Church on their sight-seeing trip.

When they sat on the stairs,

He said "Give them three chairs."

So the usher sang out "Hip, hip, hip".

Miscellaneous

Victoria, the famed British queen

Ascended the throne as a teen.

And while Monarch regnant,

She was nine times pregnant.

Her fame she achieved in between.

A trainee attorney named Shaw

Zeroed each test that he entered for.

The questions all stalled him

So everyone called him

'Necessity' for he knew no law.

A tourist strolling by the sea

When warned of the manchineal tree,

Said "I find it incredible;

Those fruits must be edible."

Now there're blisters where lips used to be.

John tried, at the Rotary bake-out,

The cute visiting member to take out.

She quickly saw through him

And sternly said to him,

"I'm here to make up, not to make out."

(Note: A Rotarian visiting
another Rotary club gets a "make
up" which gives him or her
attendance credit in his or her
own club.)

www.ingramcontent.com/pod-product-compliance
Lightning Source LLC
Chambersburg PA
CBHW040848100426
42813CB00015B/2746